Nature's Mind

poems by

Shelley Reece

Finishing Line Press
Georgetown, Kentucky

Nature's Mind

Copyright © 2022 by Shelley Reece
ISBN 978-1-64662-902-2 First Edition
All rights reserved under International and Pan-American Copyright Conventions. No part of this book may be reproduced in any manner whatsoever without written permission from the publisher, except in the case of brief quotations embodied in critical articles and reviews.

ACKNOWLEDGMENTS

With thanks to the following publications where the poems below appeared.

A Ritual to Read Together: (Woodley Memorial Press, 2013): "If a Tree Falls."
Fireweed: "Brachiopods."
Nebraska Review: "Natural Cure."
Plainsongs: "The Wyeths," "Seduction at the Oregon Coast Aquarium."
Twelve Oregon Poets ii: "The Last Hunt."

I owe much to many: to my poetry group, Barb, another Shelley, Sue, and Joe. To Portland poets and friends John Brehm, Don Colburn, Andrea Hollander, and Paulann Petersen. To the poetry staff in Pacific University's MFA in Writing. To Kwame Dawes, my first advisor in the program. A special shout out to Joe Millar, who suggested I gather my nature poems into a chapbook. To Lesley, my daughter, who knows the ins and outs of computer applications and the beauty of a well formatted document. Finally, above all, to Mary for her constantly inspiring support.

This chapbook was made possible in part by donations to the ONE LAST WORD Program. ONE LAST WORD helps to bring the last works of gifted poets to the world.

Publisher: Leah Huete de Maines
Editor: Christen Kincaid
Cover Art: Mary L. Reece
Author Photo: Lifetouch Portrait Studios Inc.
Cover Design: Elizabeth Maines McCleavy

Order online: www.finishinglinepress.com
also available on amazon.com

Author inquiries and mail orders:
Finishing Line Press
PO Box 1626
Georgetown, Kentucky 40324
USA

Table of Contents

The Harbor Overnight 1

Autumn Begins in Portland, Oregon 2

Inventory of an October Night 3

Out the Sun Room Windows 4

What Winter Does 5

The Wyeths 6

Seduction at the Oregon Coast Aquarium 7

Evening at the Beach 8

On the Margin 9

Another Nature Poem 11

The Last Hunt 12

Before Spring 13

One Spring Salamander 14

Spring, the Sweet Spring 16

Spring Fox 17

View from the Window above the River 18

Table, Fruit, Wine Jar 19

Natural Cure 20

Nightcrawlers 21

Back Garden with Girl and Frog 22

If a Tree Falls 23

A Visit to the Japanese Garden 24

Three Gardeners 25

The Garden 26

Brachiopods 28

The Hive 29

Dao Song
—Ursula K. Le Guin

O slow fish
show me the way
O green weed
grow me the way

The way you go
the way you grow
is the way
indeed

Copyright © 1974 by Ursula K. Le Guin
First appeared in WILD ANGELS, published by Capra Press in 1974
Reprinted by permission of Curtis Brown, Ltd.

The Harbor Overnight

The wave sighed
and washed away
a footprint,
leaving a window
thinner than a pane
of glass to reflect
my face in the sand.

A night moon seedling
has climbed the stairway
toward the attic
long enough ago
for vining honeysuckle
to leave a light sweetness
in the damp air.

Clockwork ratchets
its way toward midnight,
as propellers in the harbor
avoid the rocks around
the lighthouse.

Night sounds persist
a train whistles
a boat bumps against its pier
unseen aquatic animals
come up for air
breathe and submerge again.

In the morning
the salt air kisses
the water's skin
like an opening tulip.

Autumn Begins in Portland, Oregon

The cat lies in slanted sunlight
and sleeps still as death.
A crow feeds on a fox squirrel,
road kill, with four black-suited buddies watching.
They strut on the blacktop as awkward
as bowlegged cowboys in a 1930's oater.

The Japanese maples turn red,
and the yellow roses
fade from saffron. One bumble
bee has the abelia to itself.
Songbirds ravage the feeders
to store fat for long flights.

The weatherman promises
some sunny days,
but I walk gingerly
with no sudden gestures
that might throw me
into who knows how dark a winter.

Inventory of an October Night

Chilly dark.
My feet shuffle among the dry leaves.
No rain yet. Decorative grasses flourish.
I pass a raised stage where no one performs.
Moonlight radiates from the hoods of cars.
At sidewalk's end weary engines climb a hill.
An exhaust fan hums and whirs.
Outlines of leaves, some shaped like
a child's hand, color the cement.
In the distance on the upper floor
of an apartment, one small square of light
shines directly below the egg-shell moon.

Out the Sun Room Windows

The 'Midwinter Fire' Cornus rises,
its yellow leaves gone, and its leafless twigs
blush with a color too subtle to name,
—not pink, possibly dark coral—
and the bushtits throng the branches,
pecking at bits of food too small for me
to see, then crowd together on the suet,
sharing their fatty meal with chickadees
and one Townsend Warbler, the area around his eyes
streaked with yellow and brown. Birds startle
as one and perch on Cornus branches
while a squawking bluejay five times
their size lands to peck and gorge
on chunks of alabaster suet.
When he has gone, a few little birds
return to feed—song sparrows and house finches
join them, the male finches with red breasts that
complement the coral of the Cornus.
They and the towhees find the sunflower seeds
in the feeder I mean for them. I keep our old
tuxedo cat, dressed always for dinner, inside,
where he rests on the back of the blue couch, watching.

What Winter Does

The potted bamboo on our deck holds spindly canes
with dead maple leaves tangled in them,
and the wind doesn't set them free.
The burning bush is bare, having lost
its fire while we were gone for Thanksgiving.
The Cornus is a skeleton with coral bones,
and the tall black bamboo on the yard's edge
waves in the wind with remarkable grace.
The geraniums are dead, their limp leaves
now wilted lettuce.
The sun shines on the upper half
of the tallest bamboo and transforms
its leaves into a bright lime green.
Out front, my wife and a friend trim
and shape the leafless Acer palmatum
in the planter box by our front door
to help it re-discover its own form.
So that I can have something to do,
I drive three miles to our post office box,
then return with six catalogs and one monthly bill.

The Wyeths

The wind from the sea
brings ghosts of shore birds
and memories scented with evergreen
of his mother and father lying
in the distant cemetery.
A double tracked dirt road leads
away from the open window
where his mother's hands wove the tea-colored
pattern of birds in the curtains
that the breeze lets float into the room.
The painter's father rests
out there now, after being killed
by a train. In life
he was restless, and
his spirit in the wind
draws the young painter
to the window and guides
his hand over and over
in the repetitions that tempera
requires, until the picture also shows
the pressure of the old man's hand.

Seduction at the Oregon Coast Aquarium

"Sex is not straightforward in the sea."
—*Aquarium placard*

On the concrete floor
with tourists
smelling like shore life,
I stare into a round tank
that rises to the ceiling.

The glass magnifies
fourteen jellyfish:
pink, protected, gauze-like,
undulant lace
in lucent saline,
they bulge and flatten
their way through the water.

Their tendrils mime
union, trail and trap food,
and in a silent chorus,
they pulse "come hither" to me
in the old slow motion
that makes me
catch my   catch my   breath.

I am saltwater.
You are moving
inside me now.

Evening at the Beach

The sea-spray on the pines
Comes with lighthouse clockwork,
Dropping salt white speckles
On the crimson poppies
And decorating spiderweb strands.
Echoes make my hand hesitate
Over the book I'm reading,
And I check the window
To see if it's smoke or spray,
and I listen to hear if a key
scrapes in the lock or
the parrot grows restless
in the evening whisper.

On the Margin

A mind
of winter
has wind
and snow
along with
a crow
in a barren
tree
there would
have to be
a tree
even if
it was
a desert
and what
would a tree
be without
a bird in it
and a barren
tree needs
a crow
don't ask
where it
came from
(the poet's
imagination)
so now
the crow
can call
or look
for road-kill
far from
the nearest
highway

or the tree
will perhaps
bloom.

Another Nature Poem

Though I have been advised
not to write nature poems,
nature's mind says otherwise.
I sit at my desk and the crows
caw to me in the afternoon,
the Euonymus turns yellow,
and the sunlight draws
a shadow line
straight as a ruler
across the bushes.
Everywhere I look
the outdoors tells me
winter will soon arrive,
a message that falling leaves
deliver, and all varieties
of small brown birds
and black-hooded juncos
pecking extra hard for seeds
to make them fat enough
to survive the winter cold.
The rebel pink roses keep
throwing blooms. A gray squirrel
grows fat on orange rose hips.
The bamboo doesn't shed its leaves.
Buddha's expression does not change.

The Last Hunt

Quail have bodies too heavy for small wings
that leave a circle of fluted marks in snow.
Some miracle of cold holds them up.

I walked the late day hedgerows,
a hunter in the snow, dreaming.
Quail have bodies too heavy for small wings.

The steel of my shotgun, the coldest blue,
froze my hands to memories of why quail fly:
some miracle of cold holds them up.

Weeds grow where fences and hedgerows meet,
where I lifted lead boots to cross.
Quail have bodies too heavy for small wings.

They make two-note calls in a major key
and send a sentry to distract.
Some miracle of cold holds them up.

The beauty of bobwhites dancing in air
lays my gun to rest on my arm for good.
Quail have bodies too heavy for small wings.
Some miracle of cold holds them up.

Before Spring

In February living stands still.
Herbs hold their fragrance
and the rain drips
into the pot holding bamboo.
Tulip bulbs hold their place
underground, and the roses
newly trimmed mend
their stalks, cut
with gardeners' care.
Leafless twigs keep
the impulse to push out
leaves and buds.
Small birds shiver
in heavy brush.

One Spring Salamander

If you had teeth,
I'd have to move faster.

I scoop you up
into my hand,
salamander, relative,
and your feet
prickle my palm.

Pink against
your cinnamon,
I have enlarged
my way beyond you
in just a few
million years.

I might think you
content in my hand,
warming against
early spring chill. Even
the Trillium haven't opened
their trinitarian blooms
to the year.

And your head, lifted above
my mound of Venus,
lets me see you
at eye level,
alert, two black beads
threaded on either side
of your skull,
your whole body
a tube for swallowing.

I return you to the rock
where I found you
and move away fast.

Spring, the Sweet Spring

Today I feel full of juice and joy,
in no disgrace with fortune and men's eyes.
It's spring; no grieving for golden grove
unleaving. Time for maidens
to gather rosebuds,
to take pleasure's full swing,
and let bachelor buttons spread seeds
while young boys catch
falling stars from the Pleiades
and wish themselves more steadfast.

I'll watch at night and hope
golden lads and girls will live long
and happy lives like Rosacoke Mustian
and Wesley Beavers, her boyfriend,
where in North Carolina nights
they can watch the full moon
like a glowing hand-blown glass bell
full of human wishes.

Right now the bulbs are rising high
like Jesus coming back from the dead,
and the flowers' fragrances, from
Narcissus to Lilac to 'Julia Child' rose
are making all the bees besotted,
and when I smell the Zepherine
I can't refuse the drunkenness it offers.

Spring Fox

Rhododendrons flower red
as I drive in the blue dusk
up the hill to Howth Head.
I stand at the crest
looking down at Dublin
over the slanting green.
Ireland's Eye
looks back from the bay.

Near my knees, an old dog fox,
smiling the length of his snout,
flashes orange from the Scotch Broom
and bright as he is, disappears
under the yellow blooms
faster than Parnell with Kitty O'Shea.

View from the Window above the River

The spider's shadow on the window
looks like the one that twins itself
in the mirror. Out that window,
a swan climbs slowly up
from the river, its breast
high and bright, daring
the boys fishing for dabs
in the Cam to touch it.
Its wing can break a child's arm.
The shape of its body resembles
the small, clear glass swan,
a keepsake on the dresser,
sister to the big one in the river,
so delicate I can touch it only
when I'm wearing gloves,
but now I want to walk
among the butterflies
looping along the shore
and pick poppies growing there.

Table, Fruit, Wine Jar

The sweet scent of peach and apple
infuses the room with a light decay,
though I had expected the odor of must
from the Cezanne still life,
especially the dark cloth
with blue designs that spill across
the table beside the plate of fruit.
Someone interrupted by an unknown duty
left a white cloth yet to be spread, so white
it shades to blue, rumpled and dangling
from the scrolled table yet to be spread.

A pitcher apparently empty sits
as yet unfilled on the dark cloth
with wine to accompany
the afternoon, and a white
and cornflower blue bowl behind
the red and yellow globes, large and small,
waits for someone to fill it up
and overspill the day.

Natural Cure

Wedged under a fir tree
in my yard, I wrapped
with wire and cloth
a forked branch split
by wind and rain.

Bamboo leaves on the ground
rattled like corn husks
when I shifted to avoid
pine whips with needles.

A blue racer appeared.
As large as my wrist,
he torqued up and tongued the air
six inches from my face.

His beaded scales shone
like a salmon
cast up flopping
on the river rocks
under the bamboo.

He was angular as geometry,
undulant as French curves
drawn in engineering class.

A still life, he slid
without noise between leaves
that tried to rise
to their stalks.

A year later the split branch
looked exactly like the skin
on a snake's tongue
where it forks.

Nightcrawlers

They love sex in the spring grass.
Just a year after the '51 flood
the yards were full of them
every night, hermaphrodite
lovers locked together,
almost invisible in the silt,
shining back at my amber
filtered flashlight beam.
A bait station boy,
I'd hold down pair after pair
till they both relaxed,
came loose from their grip
underground,
and I could drop them
into a can. I picked up
gallons that way,
transferring them
to new dirt
in the back of the car
we came forty miles in,
just to pick them up
and sell them for bait.
I marveled at the number
that stayed coupled
tight as I dropped them
into the can with the others,
their translucent blue shining.
On my knees in strangers' yards
by night, I learned the way
desire, like water, rises from the ground.

Back Garden with Girl and Frog

No water runs in this stream
where the verdigris garden girl
holds flowers in her skirt ready
to lean down and wash the stems.
She has a patina.
(When Picasso wanted
a patina, he told his son
to pee on the goat.)
Big gray fists of dry river rock
make a lumpy mattress in the stream bed.
One foot up, four metallic salmon,
hovering, point toward a Viburnum
covered with white butterfly blossoms
that quake in every breeze
those salmon face, still in the air.
Goldfinches from a bamboo forest
pick nyjer thistle seeds, fly back,
and perch, gold leaves on black canes.
A white frog a foot high rubs
its stippled belly and laughs,
goggle eyed, at the flittering
hordes of garden bugs
a plastic frog can't eat.

If a Tree Falls

A tree fell across the yard last month,
missed the house by six inches,
and dropped in the wooded lot
next door. Maybe it was only chance,
a hundred sixty foot Douglas fir,
twenty-two inches through, falling;
it didn't damage anything, but left
its exclamation point across the lawn.
Perhaps, beyond Orion's three-star belt
and Cassiopeia's topsy-turvy chair
some celestial engineer aimed
a puff of cosmic wind as straight
as a cyclotron particle or laser light,
a perfect line in geometric space,
and the tree went down just as it should.

A Visit to the Japanese Garden

You walk through the Samurai Gate,
dip the wooden ladle into the stone bowl,
and wash away the dust from your mind.
When it is clean, you can see
that the granite chip gravel
is a pool with rhythmic waves,
and the fallen cherry blossoms
from an ancient tree refuse
to sink below the surface.
You let wisteria vines lead you
to the moon-viewing bridge,
where the slow orange-and-white koi
glide their way to the celestial falls.
The way these exotic fish kiss
the bubbles on the surface
makes you want to kiss them back.

Three Gardeners
for Mary

She sits on our garden bench some evenings,
next to the shadow of her father,
dead now nearly twenty years,
and toasts him with wine
the color of her flourishing roses,
her love of flora
which he nourished in her
being the reason she sits there
among Euonymus, rosemary, and Viburnum,
remembering when she was very small
how she followed her grandfather
through his garden, where he flicked
potato bugs from mounds of foliage
and she dispatched them with a putty knife.

The Garden

Every year fennel grows
by the faucet south of the house
taller than a man in rich soil.
It seems to season the lettuce greens
growing a few feet away.

Fifty years a gardener, my wife
plants the rest of the south side
with roses and berries then stakes
a sculptured metal kanji for "garden"
at the front. Lush blooms change
but comply with her wish.

Blueberry leaves turn red in fall.
Lavender hangs on.

Her hands hold a fertile spirit
that waves over the garden
and makes beauty rise from plain loam:
iris fronds and potato plants,
blueberry bushes and cabbage roses
peanut butter bush and latifolia.

When she sees that a flower
will face the sun, she holds it
to the light to see that it is good.

The bracken wants to grow in the shade
on the house's north side, fronds
unfurling like light green wheels.

The can yard holds plastic pots
of native plants that insist their way
into the air like cold fists
opening into a shelter for warmth.

All winter crocuses and tulips rest
in muddy torpor till the sun sucks them
from the ground to bloom
in spring's tremendous heave.

Brachiopods

Alive with secrets
and smaller than a Madeleine
these gray and gold fossils
have mouths of grooved stone
to tell their memories if I can wait

to hear how an ancient
inland sea changed
and heat hardened
even water
into desert rock.

The Hive

The roses outside my window
refuse to go away. They keep throwing blooms:
yellow, tropicana, and pink-tinged with red,
as if they can't tell it's fall,
though the weather has cooled,
the purple asters are budding,
and one variety of lavender hangs on.
The drunken bees, humming,
hovering over many blossoms,
an unreproducible geometry
fancier than a kaleidoscope,
fill pollen sacs overfull,
and, insistent, fly all
they can carry back to the hive
that grows more golden by the day.
When it turns cold, they'll brush away
the dead, drive out the drones, and begin
to fan their wings inside the hive
to warm the queen and save nectar
in their waxy combs to feed on in winter.
For the hive has nature's mind,
and preserves itself for spring.

Shelley Reece, PhD 1967 U. of Nebraska, retired from 43 years of college and university teaching as Professor of English, with 33 of those years at Portland State University—six as Director of Composition and six as Department Chair. His specialties, writing and contemporary lit, led him to the notebooks, letters, and manuscripts of the English novelist Paul Scott, author of *The Raj Quartet*. Reece's research led to a collection of Scott's ungathered essays, *My Appointment with the Muse*. Late in his teaching career, Reece became interested in adding his voice to the community of poets. After retirement, he served on the Board of The Friends of William Stafford for thirteen years, five of those years as Chair. In June, 2014, he completed an MFA in poetry from Pacific University, Forest Grove. He lived in Garden Home, a Portland, Oregon suburb, with his wife, Mary, and their rescue cat, Cardi.

www.ingramcontent.com/pod-product-compliance
Lightning Source LLC
LaVergne TN
LVHW041507070426
835507LV00012B/1392